Thunder,
The Overcomer

The story of a Long Haired, Gifted Indian Boy

By A. Kay Richardson Oxendine

This is the first of a series of books about Thunder, the Overcomer.

Thunder is a Native American Indian boy who had long hair down his back.

In school, he was teased and fell ill at one point, but he continued and pressed on, keeping his hair long all through his life.

Thunder also had special gifts, where he could help people. He made sure he always remembered these gifts and felt protected by this spirt brother Stoney.

Thunder was born in March under a full moon. He was born with a head full of hair.

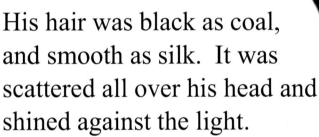

His hair was black as coal, and smooth as silk. It was scattered all over his head and shined against the light.

As soon as he was born, his parents knew that he was special, and they loved him without measure.

Thunder was not the first son to his family, however.

His older brother Stoney was never able to walk the earth. He was known only as a spirit to his family, having passed to the spirit world before being born.

Little did his family know, that Stoney would stay with Thunder all his life.

When Thunder met his grandmother for the first time, only a week old, he immediately turned his head toward the wall and began babbling, as if talking to someone. His grandmother looked in astonishment!

"Who are you talking to, grandson?" Grandmother asked as she looked toward the very blank, empty wall and then back at her grandson. But Thunder continued his stare and conversation, not understood by anyone, being that he was only a week old. But it was obvious to grandmother, that someone else was in the room.

"He sees someone," Grandmother said. "He has gifts." She smiled and kissed his forehead.

These gifts became more noticeable to others who met Thunder. His eyes would lock on certain people when they came into his space, and he would point to them and babble. At three months, he would be able to contour his eyes with great expression. He attracted other people with gifts who stated they would protect him thru his life.

Thunder's mother could not bear to cut his hair, and as it grew, discovered many different styles for her gifted son. Finally, after he was one year's old, his father decided to take him to the barber shop to have a "little boy" haircut. His mother went with them but cried as her little boys' hair was cut.

You see, Thunder was Native American, and in his culture, hair was very important to him and his tribe.

Thunder's mother believed that his hair was a physical extension of his thoughts and prayers, of his dreams and ambitions. She believed that his hair should only be cut when something changed in his life, like when someone died, or there was a significant change in his life.

Once the barber cut the hair, his mother smiled to show her son that he was beautiful no matter what, but quickly took out a bag and collected all of his hair, so she could keep her son protected. Most people thought she was crazy, but she was ok with that.

As Thunder grew older, his hair was soon down his back. He loved the fact that he was known as the boy with the long hair.

Sometimes, people would look at him and say, "Oh what a cute little girl!"

Thunder's Mom would look them straight in the eye and ask, "Where is a little girl?" She would then say, "Oh, you mean my son? Thank you!"

It never really seemed to bother Thunder that people mistook him for a girl, because he knew he was a boy and he was fine with that.

When Thunder was about three, he began to be more aggressive when it came to his gifts. When he traveled with his mother, he would always step in front of her and say, "Hold on, Mommy." At first Thunder's Mommy would laugh, but she began to notice that Thunder would protect her. Over time, he began to walk into houses and "check them out" before she walked in. His mother trusted his gifts and learned to listen to what her son told her.

Thunder would also dream magnificent dreams. He would awake and tell his mother of his dreams and together, they would interpret them. Many times, his dreams were warnings for others, and Thunder's mother would call those who Thunder dreamt about.

When Thunder was about 5 years old, his parents divorced. His mother and sister moved to a new house, while Thunder's dad stayed in his family home.

One day, while Thunder was away from his mom, somebody cut his hair. This upset him very much.

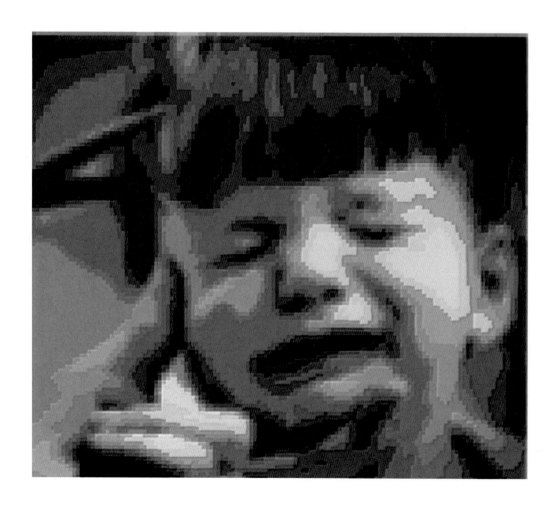

When his mother found out, she was very upset and called the person and asked them to please not touch her son's hair.

But the person did not listen.

Thunder told his Mom that the person continued to cut his hair, and thought it was funny. The person would snip a little bit of his bangs or cut a bit of the back off. Thunder begged them to stop because he knew his mother would be very upset. But the person continued.

Thunder grew angry because he told his Mom that the person would not listen to him, and he didn't understand why they would purposely do this.

Thunder's mother realized that not everyone understood his gifts, and that sometimes people would try to bring negativity to him, to alter his gifts.

Thunder's mother sat him down and prayed with him. She then told him that the only way they could stop this person from cutting his hair, was to remove his hair from their touch. Thunder's mother explained that his hair would grow back, but right now, with this new person being in his life, that they needed to stop the action that was happening to him.

Thunder allowed his mother to braid his hair, and it was so long it touched the top of his butt! She then prayed again with her son, and together they cut his braid to the back base of his head. His mother then took the braid and wrapped it in the cloth they had prayed over and put it away with tobacco and sage. She then put it in a safe place.

His mother cried and Thunder told her that her it would be ok, and he hugged her. She then took her son to a hairdresser and got him a very styled cut.

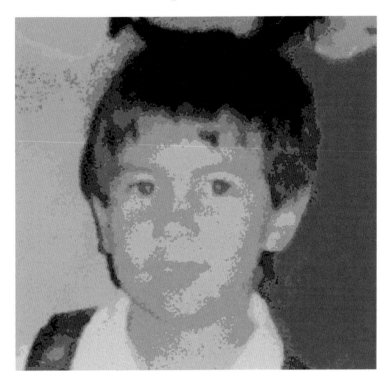

After this happened, Thunder vowed that no one would ever touch his hair again.

And they never did.

Within 3 years, Thunder's hair was back down his back again. It stayed this way, as he grew, and he enjoyed being known as the long-haired boy!

When Thunder was about 10 years old, he asked his mother about his brother Stoney. She was surprised that he brought him up, and asked, "Why are you asking, son?"

He said, "Because that is why I am never afraid. Stoney is always with me." With this he smiled, and his mother smiled too.

Thunder knew that Stoney would always be with him, watching over him, as his guardian angel.

Thunder also asked about getting baptized at his church. When the preacher asked Thunder why he wanted to do this, he stated, "Because I don't want to go to hell." Taking aback, the preacher said, "Well then we must do this."

Because of his long hair, Thunder was teased all the time. But he told his Mom that he would pray for those that said bad things to him. Sometimes, grown people would bully him too. He told his Mom maybe they were just sad, so they needed to be loved a little bit more.

When Thunder was in elementary school, he gave his apple to his teacher each day. One day, the teacher reported this behavior to his Mom. Confused, his Mom asked, "Well, what exactly is wrong?"

The teacher said, "Well, he has to eat his lunch himself and not give it away!"

Thunder's Mom explained that he meant no harm and he probably thought that maybe she was hungry. She asked the teacher, "Do you eat with him and his classmates?"

The teacher thought for a moment and said, "Why no, I don't."

"Well maybe if he sees you eat, he will not think you are hungry," Thunder's Mom said.

When Thunder's Mom asked him about it, he said, "Well, she's a teacher and she's nice, and I thought all teachers liked apples." This made his mother laugh. Thunder continued, "Not all the kids are nice to her, so I just want her to smile, Mom."

Thunder's Mom did not discourage this behavior to her son. She was happy that he had a giving heart.

When Thunder was in middle school, he began having horrible headaches and stomachaches. They became so bad that his mother began homeschooling him. With his homeschooling, he excelled and was able to return to high school and graduate with his diploma.

Overcoming so much in his life gave Thunder more confidence, and he was accepted into many colleges, where he flourished beyond measure.

To this day, Thunder's hair is still long, all the way down his back. His brother Stoney remains with him, and Thunder loves the fact that no one else can see his big brother but him.

Made in the USA
Columbia, SC
04 October 2022

68603542R00015